LET'S PLAY! LITTLE CHAMPS

ICE HOCKEY

KIM THOMPSON

NorwoodHouse Press

Cataloging-in-Publication Data

Names: Thompson, Kim, 1970-.
Title: Ice hockey / Kim Thompson.
Description: Buffalo, NY : Norwood House Press, 2026. | Series: Let's play! little champs | Includes glossary and index.
Identifiers: ISBN 9781978577312 (pbk.) | ISBN 9781978577329 (library bound) | ISBN 9781978577336 (ebook)
Subjects: LCSH: Hockey--Juvenile literature. | Hockey players--Juvenile literature.
Classification: LCC GV847.25 T474 2026 | DDC 796.962--dc23

Published in 2026 by
Norwood House Press
2544 Clinton Street
Buffalo, NY 14224

Designer: Rhea Magaro

Photo credits: Cover, p. 1 Dardalnna/Shutterstock.com; pp. 5, 7 Sergey Novikov/Shutterstock.com; ; p. 9 Lorraine Swanson/Shutterstock.com; p. 11 Sergey Spritnyuk/Shutterstock.com; p. 13 Oleksandr Osipov/Shutterstock.com; p. 14 Lucky Business/Shutterstock.com; pp. 17, 18 Oleksandr Osipov/Shutterstock.com; pp. 19, 21 Click Images/Shutterstock.com

Printed in the United States of America

CPSIA compliance information: Batch #CWNHP26: For further information contact Norwood House Press at 1-800-237-9932.

TABLE OF CONTENTS

What Is Ice Hockey?

Ice hockey is a fun sport. Players wear special ice skates with short, curved blades. They carry sticks to help them shoot a **puck** into a **goal**.

15

The Uniform

Ice hockey is fast and rough. Protective gear keeps players safe.

Padded pants are called breezers. Under their jerseys, players wear shoulder pads. There are more pads for the elbows and **shins**. Gloves protect the hands.

Players must wear helmets. Most hockey helmets include a cage that covers the face.

Hockey **goalies** need extra protection. They wear special gloves. They wear thick padding on their legs, chest, and arms.

02

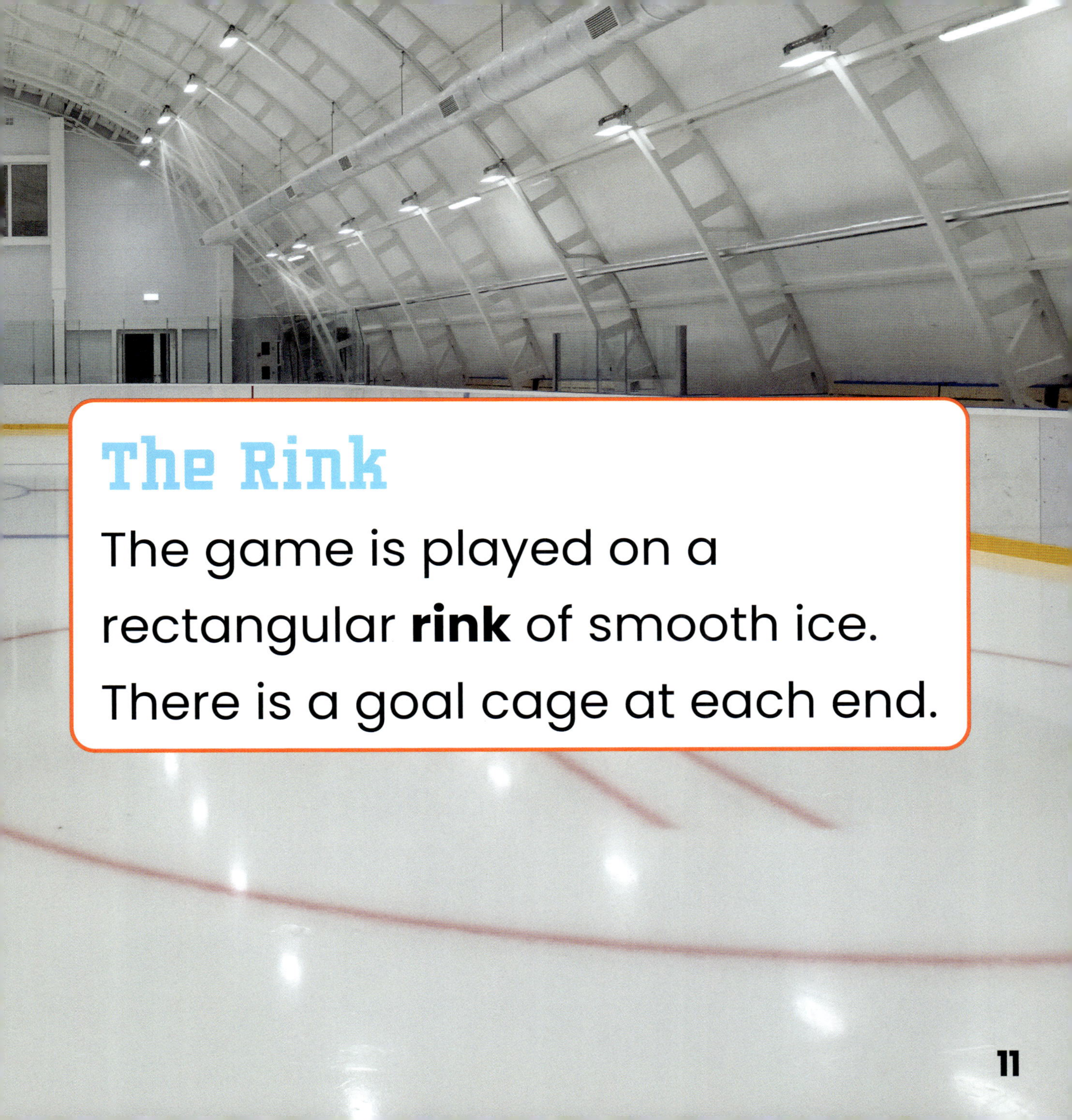

The Rink

The game is played on a rectangular **rink** of smooth ice. There is a goal cage at each end.

Rules of the Game

A **face-off** at the center of the rink begins the game. An official drops the puck between a player from each team. The players use their sticks to try to gain control of the puck for their team.

The team in control of the puck is the **offense**. They try to shoot the puck into the other team's goal to score a point. The other team is the **defense**. They try to block the offense.

Positions on the Team

Each team has six players on the ice. Three are **forwards**. They work together to get the puck past the goalie and into the goal.

Two defensive players **assist** the goalie. They block the other team's shots.

Each team's goalie stays near their goal box. Goalies try to keep the puck out of the goal. They can use their hands as well as their sticks.

How to Be Game-Ready

Players should eat healthy foods like fruits, vegetables, and lean meats. They should drink plenty of water. Getting enough sleep gives them energy to play their best.

GLOSSARY

assist (uh-SIST): to help another player on your team

defense (dee-FENS): the team that tries to stop the other team from scoring

face-off (FAYS-awf): when an official drops the puck between a player from each team; the players use their sticks to battle for control of the puck

forwards (FOR-wurdz): players whose main job on a team is to score points

goal (gohl): the net that players try to shoot the puck into to score a point

goalies (GOH-leez): players who guard the goal and try to keep the puck from going in

offense (AW-fens): the team that has control of the puck and tries to score

puck (puhk): the small, flat, round piece of rubber that players hit with their sticks in ice hockey

rink (ringk): an enclosed area with a smooth surface that is used for skating

shins (shinz): the front parts of your legs between your knees and ankles

THINKING QUESTIONS

1. How do ice hockey players use their sticks?
2. Describe one piece of protective gear that ice hockey players wear.
3. What is a face-off?
4. What is the job of the offense?
5. How do goalies help their teams?

INDEX

ABOUT THE AUTHOR

Kim Thompson is a writer, mom, and sports fan from Columbus, Ohio. She loves to watch athletes' amazing skills on the court, field, or diamond. She believes that all kids should try out the sports that interest them and always remember to have fun!